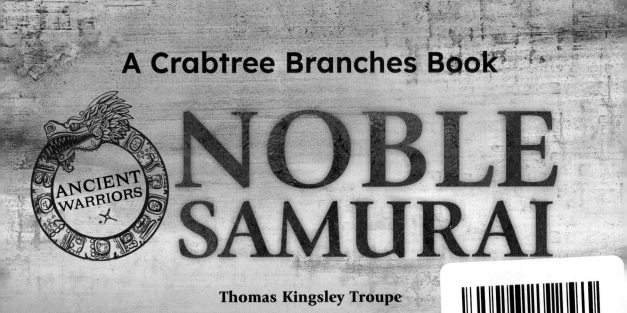

A Crabtree Branches Book

ANCIENT WARRIORS

NOBLE SAMURAI

Thomas Kingsley Troupe

Crabtree Publishing
crabtreebooks.com

School-to-Home Support for Caregivers and Teachers

This high-interest book is designed to motivate striving students with engaging topics while building fluency, vocabulary, and an interest in reading. Here are a few questions and activities to help the reader build upon his or her comprehension skills.

Before Reading:
- *What do I think this book is about?*
- *What do I know about this topic?*
- *What do I want to learn about this topic?*
- *Why am I reading this book?*

During Reading:
- *I wonder why...*
- *I'm curious to know...*
- *How is this like something I already know?*
- *What have I learned so far?*

After Reading:
- *What was the author trying to teach me?*
- *What are some details?*
- *How did the photographs and captions help me understand more?*
- *Read the book again and look for the vocabulary words.*
- *What questions do I still have?*

Extension Activities:
- *What was your favorite part of the book? Write a paragraph on it.*
- *Draw a picture of your favorite thing you learned from the book.*

TABLE OF CONTENTS

On the Battlefield

The samurai rides his horse along the hilltop. He stops and surveys the valley below. Other samurai from his clan join him.

The warlord raises a flag to the sky. The other samurai shout their battle cries. They draw their weapons and race downhill to fight their enemy.

What's a Samurai?

The samurai were a class of warriors from ancient Japan. They belonged to a **caste**, or group of people, based on their wealth.

At first, the samurai served great lords called *daimyo*, fighting their enemies and protecting their lands. Later, they became part of the ruling class under one military leader, the *shogun*.

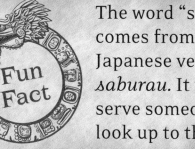

Fun Fact

The word "samurai" comes from the Japanese verb *saburau*. It means "to serve someone and look up to them."

A samurai lived by a special code called *bushido*. Also known as the way of the warrior, bushido described the importance of loyalty, honor, and **martial arts**.

Samurai who committed crimes and were sentenced to death were allowed the suicide ritual called *seppuku*. By slicing open their own stomach, they restored their honor.

Samurai History & Life

The first samurai warriors appeared in 10th century Japan. They were used to fight alongside Japanese armies during early **medieval** times.

Over time, these warriors rose in power. The years 1185-1868 were known as the Age of the Samurai. Japan was governed by these warriors under the shogun during this period.

New samurai started training before the age of five. Their first sword was made of wood. They got their first real blade between the age of five and seven.

Samurai were trained to fight with and without weapons. They learned to ride horses and use a bow and arrow.

Fun Fact

Samurai learned to survive in many conditions. Physical conditioning included going days without food or standing in deep snow with little clothing on.

Samurai Clothing

When a samurai was not training or engaged in battle, he usually wore a *kimono*. It is a traditional Japanese robe that is sewn in a "T" shape.

The kimono is tied at the front with an *obi*, or belt. When a samurai walked around town, he usually wore a large hat to conceal his face.

For battle, a samurai wore a helmet called a *kabuto*. The helmet had a crest on the front and iron scales all around it. The helmet of a leader would be **elaborately** decorated so he could be seen from the battlefield.

Fun Fact

A samurai's leg armor protected the warrior's thighs and upper legs. It looked similar to a skirt, and was designed to protect a **cavalry** rider's legs from attack.

A samurai also wore armor on his **torso**, arms, and legs. The breastplate, called a *dou*, was covered with iron pieces to protect him from swords and arrows.

Samurai Weapons

The main weapon used by a samurai was a *katana*. A katana is a curved sword with a single-edged blade. A square guard above the handle protects the samurai's hands.

The katana's long grip was made for the warrior to hold the weapon with two hands. The katana was often stored inside a **sheath** and worn on the belt.

Fun Fact

Some katanas were custom-made for the samurai who wielded it. The sword's owner and the battles they fought in can be determined by the designs on the blade.

Samurai also fought in battles with long bows, or *yumi*. Fighting with a bow on horseback was called *kyuba no michi*.

The bows were made of bamboo and finished with **lacquer**. Some arrows were powerful enough to pierce armor or the planks of an enemy's boat.

Samurai Fighting

Samurai battles could be brutal and bloody. As skilled warriors who followed the *bushido*, it was more honorable to die than be defeated.

Sword duels between two warriors from opposing clans happened during large battles. They would face each other and draw their swords quickly and attack.

Born in 1584, Miyamoto Musashi was one of the most famous samurai. He fought in over 60 duels between 1604-1613 and was never defeated.

Musashi was known as one of the finest swordsmen in the country. He created his own sword style and wrote popular books on fighting strategy.

Fun Fact

At age 13, Musashi challenged an older samurai named Arima Kihei. Kihei had insulted Musashi and treated him like a child. Musashi threw him down and defeated him with a wooden staff.

Samurai Today

Where are all of the samurai today? In 1868, **Emperor** Meiji replaced the shogun as the leader of Japan. The new leadership changed Japan and the samurai faded away.

Stories of samurai have appeared in movies, books, and video games. Tourists can visit Samurai Museum in Japan to learn more about these honorable fighters.

Fun Fact

A samurai's sword is often described as his soul. This made his sword the most important thing he owned.

The samurai are remembered for their swordsmanship and code of behavior. Some of the greatest achievements in weaponry were developed for the samurai in ancient Japan. Today, martial arts in Japan still includes the study of bushido.

Tales of their battles and duels and way of living have long been featured in books and movies. The samurai will always be remembered as the most noble and deadly ancient warriors!

Glossary

caste (KAST) A system that divides people into separate groups by wealth or rank

cavalry (KA-vuhl-ree) Soldiers mounted on horseback, also in moving vehicles or helicopters

elaborately (ih-LAB-uh-ruht-lee) With a lot of artistic detail

emperor (EM-pr-ur) The ruler of an empire

lacquer (LA-kr) A liquid material like varnish that dries quickly into a shiny layer

martial arts (MAAR-shuhl aarts) Fighting skills that people practice for battle, sports, or self-defense

medieval (MED-ee-vuhl) The period in European history that came between ancient and modern times

sheath (SHEETH) A case for a blade or sword

torso (TAWR-so) The middle part of the human body

Index

Websites to Visit

https://www.youtube.com/watch?v=2opogq3QsNY
[Video of history of samurai]

https://www.metmuseum.org/art/online-features/metkids/explore/22506/Japanese-Armor-Yoroi

https://online.kidsdiscover.com/unit/samurai

About the Author

Thomas Kingsley Troupe is the author of over 200 books for young readers. When he's not writing, he enjoys reading, playing video games, and investigating haunted places with the Twin Cities Paranormal Society. Otherwise, he's probably taking a nap or something. Thomas lives in Woodbury, Minnesota, with his two sons.

Written by: Thomas Kingsley Troupe
Designed by: Bobbie Houser
Series Development: James Earley
Proofreader: Kathy Middleton
Educational Consultant: Marie Lemke M.Ed.

Photographs:
istock: GCShutter: p. 12-13; davidf: p. 15
Shutterstock: djgis: cover, p. 1; zef art: p. 4-5; metamorworks: p. 5, 9, 28-29; Total art: p. 6-7, 16; oneinchpunch: p. 8; Travel Drawn: p. 10-11; Aleksey Mnogosmyslov: p. 14; siriwat sriphojaroen: p. 17; Kostiantyn: p. 18-19; Avesun: p. 20; Josiah_S: p. 21; KaiJaeArt: p. 22-23; beibaoke: p. 24-25; Vassamon Anansukkasem: p. 26-27

Crabtree Publishing

crabtreebooks.com   800-387-7650
Copyright © 2024 Crabtree Publishing

Printed in the U.S.A./072023/CG20230214

Published in Canada
Crabtree Publishing
616 Welland Ave.
St. Catharines, Ontario
L2M 5V6

Published in the United States
Crabtree Publishing
347 Fifth Ave
Suite 1402-145
New York, NY 10016

Library and Archives Canada Cataloguing in Publication
Available at Library and Archives Canada

Library of Congress Cataloging-in-Publication Data
Available at the Library of Congress

Hardcover: 978-1-0398-0947-5
Paperback: 978-1-0398-1000-6
Ebook (pdf): 978-1-0398-1106-5
Epub: 978-1-0398-1053-2